THE LITTLE ONE'S LOG

The LITTLE ONE'S LOG

Baby's Record

by
Eva Erleigh

With Foreword by
Dr Eric Pritchard

Illustrated by
Ernest H. Shepard

rh
BOOKS

DEDICATED

TO

JOAN AND ELIZABETH ANN

Contents

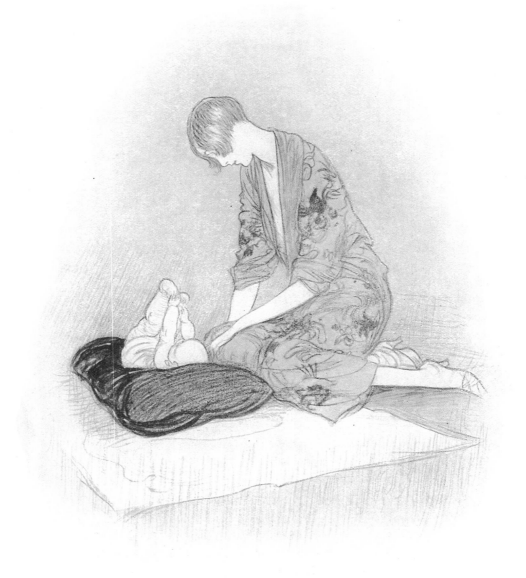

Foreword

IF every mother kept a record of her children's progress of the kind rendered so easy and interesting by the use of this little diary, I feel sure that my brethren of the medical profession would feel extremely thankful.

The diagnosis and treatment of conditions of illness in children are greatly facilitated by accurate knowledge of their previous health and physical development, but unless a written record has been kept information on these points is usually unreliable and fragmentary.

I am glad of this opportunity of expressing my appreciation of the manner in which the

FOREWORD

Authoress of these annals has fulfilled her task. I believe the information contained within its pages is substantially correct, and that the advice afforded is in accordance with sound principles of Mothercraft. Those who keep an accurate record of the events in their children's lives, on the lines for which provision is made in the attractive pages of this little volume, will assuredly meet with their reward.

ERIC PRITCHARD, 1927

Preface

THIS book supplies only a framework to be filled in by the mother who will write the record of her child. It is in reality her book, not mine. I have simply ventured to suggest the form which that record should take, and to indicate points that experience has taught me are likely to be of special value and interest in the future.

A mother does not anticipate that she will ever forget any events in the life of her child, yet in later years some do come to be forgotten or only partially remembered. A short note of the time and manner of such little things as a nasty fall, a phase of restlessness or night terrors, may afterwards prove invaluable in throwing light on some physical or mental disturbance. It is just the point that is most easily forgotten which subsequently proves the most important. But

PREFACE

such a record, to be of value, must be accurate, and I would therefore strongly advise that events should be entered in this book at the time of their occurrence.

I have endeavoured to provide a few notes that may be helpful, to supply criteria from which judgments may be deduced, and to point the way along the path laid down by modern science and modern knowledge, and I have been at pains to base my text upon information generally accepted as sound and correct to-day.

I have to thank Dr. Eric Pritchard for his kindness in writing a foreword, and I am deeply indebted to him and also to Miss Liddiard, Matron of the Mothercraft Training Society, Dr. Elizabeth Sloan Chesser, Dr. Hector Cameron and Dr. Elmslie, for their kind interest and helpful criticism.

EVA ERLEIGH, 1927

The Little One's Log

Weight. THE average weight of a boy baby at birth is seven and a half pounds, that of a girl baby seven pounds and one ounce. There are variations above and below this figure, for a child may weigh as little as six pounds, or as much as ten pounds, and still be healthy, provided height and other details are in proportion.

Height. The average height of a boy baby at birth is twenty-one inches, of a girl slightly less. This seldom varies, but it is important to note any departure from normal.

Feeding. There can be no doubt that the best food for a baby is its mother's milk. Cow's milk can be made to resemble mother's milk, but is never identical, for mother's milk contains certain properties that cannot be reproduced artificially. Moreover, nothing has yet been found to take the place of colostrum, which is secreted by the

Born at..

On the................day of...19........ at ....m.

to..

Physician   Nurse

Weight   Height   No. of feeds in
                                                    twenty-four hours

Feeding

breasts during the first few days of baby's life, before the true milk appears. When it is understood, for instance, that calves do not thrive as well when they are given milk other than that of the cow that gave birth to them, it is easily realised how vitally important it is that the baby should receive his mother's milk. Nearly every mother can nurse her baby; it is exceptional to be unable to do so, and if difficulties arise they are more often due to want of observance of the technique of correct nursing, than to any defect in the milk. If artificial feeding has to be resorted to, modified cow's milk is undoubtedly the best, and patent foods of any kind should not be used except under a doctor's orders.

A baby should be fed every three hours, and no feeds should be given at night, that is, between ten p.m. and six a.m.; absolute regularity is most important. The large baby of nine or ten pounds will sometimes do better if fed only every four hours. Plain boiled water, without any addition of sugar, can be given with advantage from a bottle or spoon, between feeds. A baby may cry from thirst without being actually hungry.

General Development. A new-born baby should be kept as quiet as possible and sleep twenty hours out of the twenty-four. Baby needs warmth, but also plenty of

fresh air, and should be out of doors as much as possible, for sunshine and air are as necessary to a growing baby as to a growing plant. When he is in a perambulator, the hood should be kept down except in very bad weather; when the sun is very bright, a shade should be provided.

Regularity is one of the most important factors in the successful management of a baby, and he should be trained from the first to have regular bowel movements every day—these should take place two or three times daily at the same time each day.

Absolute cleanliness in baby's surroundings is, of course, essential, and it is impossible to over-estimate the importance of the nurse possessing perfect health and a happy, gentle disposition.

BABY'S FIRST PHOTOGRAPH

On the.............................day of..19........

the name of...

was bestowed on baby according to the rites of..............................

....

Godfathers　　　　　*In the presence of*　　　　　*Godmothers*

Presents received　　　　　　　　　*From*

17

RECORD OF PROGRESS DURING THE FIRST THREE MONTHS OF BABY'S LIFE

Weight.   The average weight of a three-months old baby is about twelve pounds, the normal increase in weight for the first three months being one and a half pounds per month; a small baby may increase in weight more rapidly, and a large baby more slowly. An average gain of five ounces to eight ounces a week is good, and it is better for the increase in weight to be steady than to fluctuate. A baby gaining ten ounces a week for several weeks in succession is most probably being over-fed.

Feeding.   The average quantity of breast milk, or its equivalent, required by a baby of four weeks old is fifteen to eighteen ounces in twenty-four hours, or two and a half to three ounces at each of six three-hourly feeds. This amount should be increased by four ounces for the twenty-four hours

RECORD OF PROGRESS DURING THE FIRST
THREE MONTHS OF BABY'S LIFE

Weight :

    At one month ....

    At two months ....

    At three months ....

Feeding :

    At one month ....

    At two months ....

    At three months ....

Digestion :

Average number of hours spent out of doors each day...........................

      ,,   ,,   *in sleep*...

every month, in amounts of one ounce each week. To ascertain the quantity taken by a breast-fed baby, the baby should be weighed with all its clothes on immediately before and after each feeding for twenty-four hours. A small quantity of orange juice should be given daily to all bottle-fed babies.

General Development

Physical.

Baby should be allowed ample exercise every day. Both before the morning bath and before the evening wash his napkins should be undone so that he may stretch and kick, for exercise is necessary from the earliest age for the proper development of the muscles. Most authorities are agreed that a baby should never wear what are known as " long clothes," but if baby is so clothed, he should certainly be short-coated by the time he is three months old. He should spend at least four hours a day out of doors, and longer, if possible. If there is a garden, he should be out all day.

Mental.

When baby is about two months old, he will probably give his first conscious smile, and care should be taken not to over-stimulate the brain, for quiet is very essential at this age, and objects should not be dangled before his eyes, or too many attempts made to attract his attention or provoke his smile.

GENERAL DEVELOPMENT

PROGRESS AT SIX MONTHS

Weight.
At six months old the average baby (weighing seven and a half pounds at birth) should have doubled his birth-weight; that is, he should weigh between fifteen and sixteen pounds.

Feeding.
If baby has been fed at three-hourly intervals, when he is four months old these should be changed to four-hourly, the times between the feedings being lengthened gradually, for with a baby it is never wise to change anything suddenly. About seven ounces each feed is the normal quantity of food required at six months (i.e. about thirty-five ounces for twenty-four hours).

General Development
Physical.
Baby should now sleep about sixteen to eighteen hours out of the twenty-four. Longer time should be given every day for exercise; baby should lie on a cushion or in a play pen for about fifteen minutes three times a day, and be free to kick or roll with the napkins removed. He will

22

PROGRESS AT SIX MONTHS

Weight :

At four months ....

At five months ....

At six months ....

Feeding :

At four months ....

At five months ....

At six months ....

Digestion :

Number of hours spent out of doors each day ....

,, ,, *in sleep* ....

first try to hold his head up when about four months old.

Mental.   At four months old baby will grasp objects with his hands, but the eye and hand still work very imperfectly together. He will put many objects in his mouth, as his sense of taste is more developed than his sense of touch or sight.

CARE OF THE TEETH

The age at which baby cuts his first teeth varies considerably ; six months is the average, but some babies who are in every way healthy do not cut them until eight or nine months old. Six to eight teeth at one year old, and twenty at two years are normal. Retarded dentition is a symptom of rickets, and should not be regarded lightly.

The order in which the teeth make their appearance is of no great consequence. When baby has about eight teeth, they should be brushed night and morning with a soft brush, using plain bicarbonate of soda, or milk of magnesia, as a dentifrice. It is unwise to wash the mouth of a baby with glycerine and boracic or any other substance, unless he has thrush. Breast feeding is the best way to insure sound teeth and proper development of the jaws.

Never allow the use of a dummy or comforter ; these deform the mouth by pushing out the front teeth and pushing up the palate,

CUTTING OF FIRST TEETH

DATE.   DATE.

1   1
2   2
3   3
4 ....   UPPER   4
5   5

RIGHT.   LEFT.

DATE.   RIGHT.   LEFT.   DATE.

1   1
2 ....   LOWER.   2
3   3
4   4
5   5

Usual age of cutting

NAME OF TOOTH.	LOWER.	UPPER.
1. *Central Incisor*	6–8 months.	8–12 months.
2. *Lateral Incisor*	12–16 ,,	8–12 ,,
3. *Canine (Eye Tooth)*	18–20 ,,	18–20 ,,
4. *First Molar*	12–16 ,,	12–16 ,,
5. *Second Molar*	24–32 ,,	24–32 ,,

Number of teeth :

At one year   ....

At two years   ....

and may even cause adenoids. Thumb sucking is equally bad for the formation of the mouth, and the habit should never be allowed to form.

Train baby from birth to sleep with his mouth shut, for by encouraging nose breathing the correct formation of the mouth will be much helped. It is important, after baby is seven months old, to give him hard crusts and baked bread or a bone to gnaw; these are best given before meals when the child is hungry. The jaws cannot develop properly unless they are exercised, and if the jaws are undeveloped the permanent teeth will be overcrowded. An apple is the best possible cleanser of the teeth; one should be peeled whole and baby allowed to nibble at it. This gives excellent exercise to the jaws.

It is particularly important that a child should not eat bread or biscuits before going to bed, as particles of starch may adhere to the teeth and undergo fermentation during the night, with the production of acids which erode the teeth.

A child should be taken to a dentist when he is four years old, and subsequently regularly every six months. Faulty formation of the teeth can be rectified when young, and first teeth that are decayed produce poison and may cause digestive troubles, or infect the tonsils.

BABY'S TEETH

First visit to the dentist :

Remarks :

Cutting of second teeth :

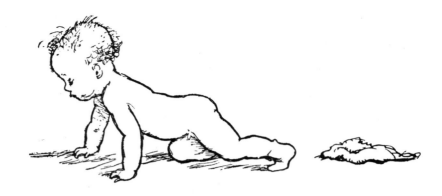

PROGRESS AT NINE MONTHS

Weight.

At nine months old the average weight of a baby is about eighteen-and-a-half to nineteen pounds.

Feeding.

At seven months old a baby needs some addition to the milk diet he has been receiving. This should take the form of hard crusts, rusks and wholemeal bread baked in an oven, which should be given before feeds two or three times a day.

At eight months small quantities of oatmeal jelly or barley jelly should be given before the milk feeds. This can be mixed with a little milk and given from a spoon so as to teach baby to eat. It is wisest to start with very small quantities at first, —later, one of the jellies with the addition of a little milk can form a whole meal. The daily orange juice should be continued throughout childhood.

At eight or nine months old weaning should

PROGRESS AT NINE MONTHS

Weight :

    At seven months ....

    At eight months ....

    At nine months ....

Feeding :

    At seven months ....

    At eight months ....

    At nine months ....

Digestion :

Number of hours spent out of doors each day ....

    ,,   ,,   *in sleep* ....

definitely commence. It is as important to wean from the bottle if the child is artificially fed, as from the breast, since prolonged sucking is very detrimental to good mouth formation. By the end of the ninth month all bottles should be given up, except for the ten o'clock feed (p.m.).

General Development.

Physical.

From seven months onwards a play-pen is a most useful means of providing exercise for baby. In it he can roll and kick in safety, learn to pull himself up to a sitting position by the bars, and, at about nine months old, make his first efforts in crawling. It is also advisable to accustom a child to being left alone for short periods, and in a play-pen he can come to no harm. A mattress placed in the pen will keep the child from floor draughts and prevent him from hurting himself. In the summer it can be placed in the garden or on a balcony, for it is important both that the child should be out of doors and that he should have plenty of opportunity for exercise.

Mental.

From seven months onwards baby should be able to control his hands, grasp objects securely, take pleasure in soft, woolly toys, india-rubber balls, rag dolls, etc. He will probably commence to make his first efforts at speech between seven and nine months old.

BABY'S FIRST BIRTHDAY

Weight.

At one year the average baby should weigh between twenty-one and twenty-two pounds.

Height.

The average height is about thirty-one inches.

Feeding.

At ten months old a little milk pudding, baked apples or prune pulp should be given at the midday meal. Mashed potatoes and red gravy, or vegetable or mutton broth may also be introduced. At eleven months the yolk of an egg may be given, a teaspoonful only at first. It is wise to commence with very small amounts of each new food and to give only one course at the midday meal, either milk pudding or gravy and potato, etc. Barley or oatmeal jelly, with milk to drink, may form breakfast and tea. A drink of milk may be given at ten p.m. if baby wakes, but he should now be gradually weaned from the ten p.m. meal, and accustomed to four meals only a day.

General Development.

Physical.

Baby should sleep fifteen hours out of the twenty-four; twelve are usual at night, two in the morning and one in the afternoon. If baby is well

BABY'S FIRST BIRTHDAY

Weight :

    At ten months ....

    At eleven months ....

    At twelve months ....

Height :

    At one year ....

Feeding :

    At ten months ....

    At eleven months ....

    At twelve months ....

Digestion :

Number of hours spent out of doors each day ....

    ,,   ,,   *in sleep* ....

35

trained, napkins may be partly dispensed with about the ninth month, and when he is one year old should no longer be necessary.

Some babies start walking when they are a year old, but many not until they are fourteen or fifteen months, and there is no cause for anxiety, so long as the limbs are strong and firm to the touch and he attempts to crawl; but if a child does not attempt to walk by the time he is eighteen months old, a doctor should be consulted.

Mental.

When a year old, baby should be able to speak a few words distinctly and understand a great part of what is said to him. It is not wise to talk baby language to him, as, being highly imitative, he learns entirely through imitation.

BABY'S FIRST STEPS

The average age for baby to start to walk is from twelve to fifteen months. A baby should be allowed to walk when he shows a desire to do so, and no effort should be made to teach him artificially before that time. He will have learned before then to pull himself up on his legs in various ways and will have gradually strengthened his muscles, and if plenty of exercise has been allowed in infancy, and he has received a correct diet, his flesh should feel firm and springy to the touch and he will be in good condition.

Care should be taken, if the child is heavy, that he is not on his feet for too long at a time. Throughout childhood children should not be kept too long in any one position but be allowed freedom in their movements, and it will be observed that they will alternately run, walk, lie

BABY'S FIRST STEPS

On the ....day of ....19........

Age..

REMARKS

down, roll or swing, thus bringing all muscles into play and never using any one for a long period, which is far best for their development.

As a child grows older it is a mistake to keep him too much in a perambulator. A good plan is to allow two or three runs during the morning alternating with rests in the perambulator, in order that the child may not be too long in one position. This should commence when he is about two years old.

Many children do not develop a sure sense of balance until six or seven years old, and therefore are unable to ride a toy bicycle, walk a plank, etc., until then.

Any tendency to flat feet should be corrected by simple tip-toe exercises, attention to correct foot-wear, and the riding of toys propelled by pedals. Bad walking is often caused by flat feet, the toes being turned very much out or excessively in, in which case a doctor should be consulted. Very stiff soles may also cause excessive turning in or out of the toes, and shoes should be tested to see if they bend readily under the child's weight.

Riding should be indulged in sparingly with young children, as too much may cause bow legs and deformities of the pelvis. Ballet dancing is apt to cause deformity in the feet and also in the legs and pelvis, in young children.

40

PROGRESS AT EIGHTEEN MONTHS

Weight.

    The average weight at eighteen months is twenty-four to twenty-five pounds.

Feeding.

    At eighteen months a little fish or chicken can be commenced, but should not be given more often than three times a week. Green vegetables should be added to the diet from about the thirteenth month, and porridge, cream of wheat, etc., may gradually replace jellies for breakfast.

Wholemeal bread should always be used for children and wholemeal flour for their cakes and puddings. Fresh fruit daily is most necessary for young children, as also fresh lettuce, watercress, etc. These can be finely chopped when first given. Margarine should never be allowed to

PROGRESS AT EIGHTEEN MONTHS

Weight :

At fourteen months ....

At sixteen months ....

At eighteen months ....

Feeding :

Digestion :

Number of hours spent out of doors each day ....

   ,,   ,,   *in sleep*..

43

replace butter. Some form of cod-liver oil should be added to the diet daily during the winter months.

General Development.

Physical.

By eighteen months the average baby should be trotting about quite firmly on his feet. He should be able to feed himself with a spoon and pusher—though, of course, not without supervision and occasional help—and to drink unaided from a cup or mug. His vocabulary should be considerably increased, and he should start to use little sentences.

Mental.

The rate at which the power of speech develops varies very greatly. Slowness in learning to speak need not occasion anxiety if it is clear that the child is as quick as most to understand what is said to him.

44

BABY'S SECOND BIRTHDAY

The child of two years should weigh about twenty-eight pounds. The average height is thirty-four to thirty-five inches.

Weight.

Height.

Feeding.

After two years old a child's diet should be increased. An egg may be given for breakfast two or three times a week, and meat and chicken are allowable four times a week, broth or fish being given on other days. Light suet puddings may follow a fish or broth course, and varieties of fresh fruits and simple pudding may be added to the diet. No food will be required before break-fast, and the number of meals should now be limited to three. The juice of an orange with a glass of cold water forms an excellent drink on waking.

46

BABY'S SECOND BIRTHDAY

Weight :   Height :

Feeding :

General Development.

Physical.

The two-year old child should sleep for twelve hours at night and for one and a half to two hours every morning, preferably out of doors.

Let the child be clad as lightly as possible : he will keep himself warm by exercise, for when awake he is always running about. Three garments for indoor wear should be enough, summer and winter ; during winter these should be all of wool. In the summer a child should be allowed to run about naked in the sun for short periods on warm days ; this is very beneficial, but care must be taken to protect head and eyes by a hat.

Mental.

He should use many connected sentences and be able to make himself generally understood. At this stage he is passing from babyhood to childhood, and should be becoming more independent. It is important to allow him to develop this sense and to start to train him to do little things for himself, such as to wash his hands, remove his shoes, carry objects, etc. Between the second and third year he is developing rapidly in mind and character, and much naughtiness or nervousness is caused during this time through keeping the child too much of a baby and giving him too little opportunity to develop his growing powers of body and mind. Opportunities should be made of giving him little " honourable " trusts and responsibilities, and tasks that will help others.

BIRTHDAY RECORDS

The diet of a child from three years onwards is substantially the same as that suggested for a child of two years, except that the quantities should be gradually increased as the child grows older. By the age of seven the normal child should be able to eat any plain, wholesome food. Three meals a day are amply sufficient for most children throughout childhood. At three years the child should sleep for twelve hours at night and for one hour in the morning or afternoon. He should start to dress and undress himself, and learn to carry such things as plates, etc., without breaking them. At about three and a half years old he should be able to walk up and down stairs alone, and begin to care for simple tales, scribbling with chalks, building with large bricks, and so on.

BIRTHDAY RECORDS

At three years :

    Weight.....................................

    Height ....

    General development :

Average:

    Weight : 2 stone 5 lb.

At four years :

    Weight....................................

    Height ....

    General development :

    Weight : 2 stone 8 lb.

At four years the child should start to bath himself and clean his teeth. Also he should be able to bowl a hoop and catch a ball, etc. He should still sleep or rest one hour a day, if he will, out of doors in a perambulator, but a perambulator should not be necessary otherwise.

At five years the child can start to learn his letters, tell the time and count correctly. He can learn dancing and try to skip, etc. Simple ear training and singing lessons are excellent at this time, and at five and a half he can attend a kindergarten class. He should still sleep one hour in the day and twelve at night.

At six years old the child should commence real lessons, but it is important that he should rest on his back every day to prevent round shoulders through sitting over-long. Eleven hours' sleep at night is normally required and is generally needed until nine or ten years of age. A child will often need more sleep during term time than during the holidays. It is advisable to allow him to get up as soon as he wakes in the morning, however early this may be, as this establishes a very good habit and often prevents many bad ones. Children vary very much in the amount of sleep they require, and though they should always be allowed sufficient for their needs, they should not spend longer in bed than the time

BIRTHDAY RECORDS

At five years :

Weight...

Height ....

General development :

Average :

Weight : 2 stone 12lbs.

At six years :

Weight...

Height ....

General development :

Weight : 3 stone 2lbs.

actually required for sleeping, and they should be taught to sleep with their hands under their pillows.

At seven years old a child commences to pass from the " mother phase," during which time the mother has been the chief centre and interest of his life, and it is wise for the mother to encourage the child in outside interests and to withdraw herself a little into the background in order that the child may develop self-confidence and independence. The first seven years of life are far the most impressionable, and all authorities consider that it is during those years that the foundations of a child's character are laid; certainly it is during these years that the mother has both the greatest responsibilities and the greatest opportunities.

BIRTHDAY RECORDS

At seven years :

    Weight..

    Height ....

    General development :

Average :

    Weight : 3 stone 7 lb.

PROGRESS IN THE ARTS

First Dancing Lessons   *Age*   *At*

Progress :

First Gymnastics   *Age*   *At*

Progress :

First Riding Lessons   *Age*   *At*

Progress :

PROGRESS IN THE ARTS

First Drawing Lessons   *Age*   *At*

Progress :

First Music Lessons   *Age*   *At*

Progress :

SCHOOL RECORD

First Lessons   *Age*   *At*

Progress ....

First School   *Age*   *At*

Progress ....

RELIGIOUS RECORD

First Prayer :

First Attending Divine Service :

Confirmation :

BOOKS RECOMMENDED ON THE CARE OF THE CHILD

THE MOTHERCRAFT MANUAL.

By Miss Liddiard   3s. 6d.

A most useful book for all mothers to possess, containing general principles of management, detailed directions as to clothing, cots, breast and artificial feeding, weaning, etc. Excellent tables of milk mixtures for infants, very clear and easy to follow. Deals with the child up to two years old, and is written by the Matron of the Mothercraft Training Society.

THE BOOK OF BREAST FEEDING.

By Miss Hester Viney   1s.

An invaluable book for all mothers nursing their babies. Contains directions for increasing the milk supply, for supplementary feeding and weaning, for the overcoming of any difficulties that arise when nursing, and much other useful information.

MOTHERCRAFT. Published by the National League for Health, Maternity and Child Welfare.   4s. 6d.

A collection of lectures delivered at various times under the auspices of the League by child-specialists. Mainly concerned with the physical well-being of the child ; such subjects as diet, care of the teeth, etc., being dealt with, also general principles of nursery hygiene. A very useful book to possess.

BOOKS RECOMMENDED

INFANT EDUCATION. By Dr. Eric Pritchard. 3s. 6d.

A most interesting book setting forth the principles of infant feeding, and the importance of early education of the baby in correct habits, and the line of conduct to be pursued.

PARENTHOOD AND THE NEWER PSYCHOLOGY.
By F. H. Richardson. 7s. 6d.

A most stimulating and interesting book; thoroughly practical in its outlook and treatment. Faults in management on the part of parents are fully discussed and many helpful criticisms and suggestions made. There is a most excellent chapter on sex education which all parents would do well to read.

EVERYDAY PSYCHOLOGY IN THE NURSERY.
Published by the National League for Health Maternity and Child Welfare. 1s.

Contains lectures by eminent child-psychologists. These lectures were especially arranged for mothers, and the subjects dealt with are those that frequently arise in every nursery.

THE MENTAL AND PHYSICAL WELFARE OF THE CHILD.
Edited by C. W. Kimmins, M.A., D.Sc. 6s.

There are nine contributors to this book, each of whom is a specialist in the subject dealt with. It will be found most useful by all parents. There is an excellent chapter on the feeding of the toddler, with specimen diet sheets; and a most interesting one on " Light and the Health of the Child." It includes chapters on the schoolboy and schoolgirl, an age about which little has been written for parents.

LIFE : HOW IT COMES. By Reid Heyman. 5s.

A book of elementary biology, most useful for parents as a basis for giving instruction to children, suitable for older children to read to themselves.

BOOKS RECOMMENDED

THE NEW PSYCHOLOGY AND THE PARENT.
By Dr. Crichton Miller.   6s.

An excellent book on the psychology of the child, explaining the psychological phases of the child's development, the importance of the rôle played by the mother, in particular as regards her sons, advice on sex education, etc. Perhaps especially useful to those whose children are at the ages of six or seven years, but certainly a book that should be read by all parents.

THE NERVOUS CHILD. By Dr. Hector Cameron. 7s. 6d.

This invaluable book should almost be entitled " The Normal Child." Any mother with children of about two or three years old or older will find it of the greatest help in solving the difficulties that are of such frequent occurrence at that period ; the question of bad habits, negativism, loss of appetite, the general psychological growth of the child and the consequences of wrong management are all very fully dealt with.

FOOD AND HEALTH.
By R. H. A. Plimmer and Violet D. Plimmer.   3s. 6d.

A most useful book on food values and vitamins, very simply and clearly written and of great value to any mother in the choice of food for her children. Contains an excellent diagram explaining the essential elements constituting " A square meal," and how one or more are often overlooked.

THE MIND OF THE GROWING CHILD.
Edited by Viscountess Erleigh.   5s.

A collection of lectures given from time to time by eminent authorities. Contains articles by Dr. H. C. Cameron, Dr. Crichton-Miller, Dr. Leonard Williams, and others, dealing with such subjects as fear, jealousy, the super-sensitive child, the backward child, family discipline, etc.

BOOKS RECOMMENDED

NURSING IN THE HOME.

By Dr. Stella Churchill. 3s. 6d.

A book that should be kept in every nursery medicine cupboard. Contains just the kind of information all mothers are sure to need at times.

THE PARENTS' BOOKSHELF.

Published by New Health Society. 6d.

Contains a well-selected bibliography of books dealing with all phases of child life. A very helpful guide to a mother in her choice of books.

BOTTLE FEEDING FOR INFANTS. By Mrs. Haldin. 1s.

Sets forth very clearly the methods advocated by Dr. Eric Pritchard. A very clear little book, easy to follow.

NURSERY LIFE. By The Hon. Mrs. St. Aubyn. 2s. 6d.

Contains chapters on the routine of a nursery day, useful advice for engaging a nurse, list of nursery training colleges. A section is devoted to children's ailments. A useful book for a young mother.

TODDLERS' DIET BOOK, for Mothers and Children.

Published by the National Society of Day Nurseries. 2s.

Contains most up-to-date advice on the feeding of children from two to six years of age, with varied diets, that have been carefully prepared, for the week. Each meal is properly balanced, and recipes are given for many of the dishes.

CHILD HEALTH AND CHARACTER. By Dr. Sloan Chesser.

An excellent book both on the physical and psychological side ; the two are nicely balanced and the advice given most practical and sound.

SUGGESTIONS FOR THE
CHILD'S LIBRARY

THREE YEARS OLD TO FIVE YEARS OLD.

Nursery Rhymes.

Caldecott Picture Books.

Little Black Sambo Series.

Beatrix Potter Books (Peter Rabbit, Benjamin Bunny, etc.).

The Baby's Life of Christ.   Mary F. Rolt.

When We Were Very Young.   A. A. Milne.

Winnie the Pooh.   A. A. Milne.

Now We Are Six.   A. A. Milne.

The House at Pooh Corner.   A. A. Milne.

FIVE TO SEVEN YEARS OLD.

The Child's Garden of Verses.   R. L. Stevenson.

Moonshine and Clover.   Laurence Housman.

The Doorway to Fairyland.   Laurence Housman.

Just So Stories.   Rudyard Kipling.

Play Time and Company.   E. V. Lucas.

Peacock Pie.   Walter de la Mare.

Children's Heroes Series.

Alice in Wonderland.   Lewis Carroll.

Through the Looking Glass.   Lewis Carroll.

Peter Pan in Kensington Gardens.   J. M. Barrie.

Peter Pan and Wendy.   J. M. Barrie.

Walter Crane Picture Books of Fairy Tales.

Little Brother and Little Sister.   Grimm.

Happy Prince and Other Tales.   Oscar Wilde.

Dr. Dolittle Series.

The Cradle Ship.   E. H. Howes.

SUGGESTIONS FOR THE CHILD'S LIBRARY

(continued)

SEVEN TO NINE YEARS OLD.

Songs of Innocence. W. Blake.

Joy Street Series.

The Arabian Nights.

Lives of the Hunted. E. Thompson Seton.

Wild Animals I have Known. E. Thompson Seton.

Pilgrim's Progress. John Bunyan.

Jungle Books. Rudyard Kipling.

Masterman Ready. Capt. Marryat.

Children of the New Forest. Capt. Marryat.

Treasure Island. R. L. Stevenson.

The King of the Golden River. Ruskin.

Come Hither. An Anthology. Walter de la Mare.

The Little Duke. Charlotte M. Yonge.

Stories from Homer. Rev. A. J. Church.

The Heroes. Chas. Kingsley.

The Child's Life of Christ. Mabel Dearmer.

The Wind in the Willows. Kenneth Graham.

Tanglewood Tales. Hawthorne.

Children's Blue Bird. Maeterlinck.

The Princess and the Goblin. George Macdonald.

Curdie and the Princess. George Macdonald.

At the Back of the North Wind. George Macdonald.

Nonsense Book. Lear.

Hans Andersen Fairy Tales.

The Children and the Pictures. Lady Glenconner.

The Prince and the Pauper. Mark Twain.

Uncle Remus. Artemus Ward.

The Children of Odin. Patrick Colum.

Water Babies. Chas. Kingsley.

66

SUGGESTIONS FOR THE CHILD'S LIBRARY
(continued)

NINE TO FOURTEEN YEARS OLD.

Call of the Wild. Jack London.

Tom Brown's School Days. Tom Hughes.

Jim Davis. John Masefield.

The Book of Discovery. John Masefield.

Bevis. Richard Jeffreys.

Scott's Works.

Dickens' Works.

Little Boy Lost. W. H. Hudson.

Westward Ho ! Chas. Kingsley.

Hereward the Wake. Chas. Kingsley.

The Last Days of Pompeii. Bulwer Lytton.

Harold. Bulwer Lytton.

The Last of the Barons. Bulwer Lytton.

The House of Pomegranates. Oscar Wilde.

Black Arrow. R. L. Stevenson.

Kidnapped. R. L. Stevenson.

Master of Ballantrae. R. L. Stevenson.

Cautionary Tales. Hilaire Belloc.

The Bad Child's Book of Beasts. Hilaire Belloc.

Puck of Pook's Hill. Rudyard Kipling.

Rewards and Fairies. Rudyard Kipling.

Kim. Rudyard Kipling.

Captains Courageous. Rudyard Kipling.

Children's Book of Art. Agnes Conway.

Tom Sawyer. Mark Twain.

Huckleberry Finn. Mark Twain.

The Holly Tree, and other Christmas Stories. Charles
Dickens. Illustrated by Ernest H. Shepard.

THE CHILD'S LIBRARY

Date   *Title of Book*   *By whom read*

RECORD OF AMUSING OR INTERESTING
SAYINGS

Date   *Saying*

RECORD OF AMUSING OR INTERESTING
SAYINGS

Date   *Saying*

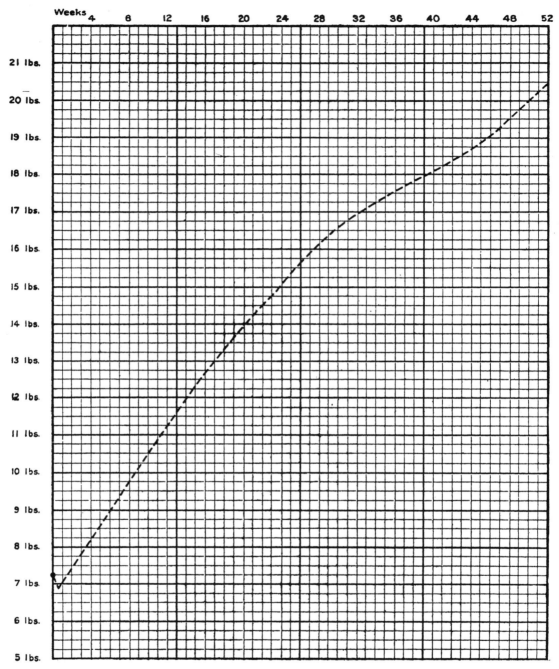

By permission of the]   [Mothercraft Training Society.

CHART SHOWING AVERAGE GAIN IN WEIGHT.

WEEKLY WEIGHT RECORD

....

....

....

....

....

....

....

....

....

....

....

....

....

....

....

....

PROGRESSIVE WEIGHT AND HEIGHT RECORD

Average Weight	Age years.	Weight.	Height.
3 stone 12 lb.	8	....	....
4 stone 5 lb.	9	....	....
4 stone 10 lb.	10	....	....
5 stone 1 lb.	11	....	....
5 stone 6 lb.	12	....	....
5 stone 11 lb.	13	....	....
6 stone 7 lb.	14	....	....
7 stone 3 lb.	15	....	....
8 stone 3 lb.	16	....	....

NOTE.—*It must be borne in mind that averages can only be approximate and are on the whole, in my experience, somewhat low and more in the nature of a minimum. It must also be remembered that girls generally weigh about 1 lb. less than boys of the same age until the age of 8 or 9 years, when they catch up the boys and outstrip them, both in weight and height, until the age of 14 or 15. After that age they increase in weight and heighth only slowly, while the boys begin to increase rapidly. I have not been able to include average heights, as I have been unable to discover sufficiently reliable statistics.*

RECORD OF VACCINATION

Date　　　　　　　　　　　　　　　*Doctor*

....　　　　　　　...

Notes

Re-Vaccination:

Date　　　　　　　　　　　　　　　*Doctor*

....　　　　　　　...

Notes

HEALTH RECORD

Notes

HEALTH RECORD

Date	Illness or Accident	Doctor

GENERAL DEVELOPMENT

SNAPSHOTS

SNAPSHOTS

SNAPSHOTS

SNAPSHOTS

BABY'S FIRST LETTER TO PARENTS

SNAPSHOTS

SNAPSHOTS

SNAPSHOTS

SNAPSHOTS

SNAPSHOTS

Published by Random House Books 2009

1 3 5 7 9 10 8 6 4 2

Text © Eva Erleigh, 1927
Illustrations © E.H. Shepard, 1927

First published in Great Britain in 1927
Reprinted in 1929, 1930, 1932, 1933 and 1935

Random House Books
Random House, 20 Vauxhall Bridge Road,
London SW1V 2SA

www.rbooks.co.uk

Addresses for companies within The Random House Group Limited
can be found at: www.randomhouse.co.uk/offices.htm

The Random House Group Limited Reg. No. 954009

A CIP catalogue record for this book
is available from the British Library

ISBN 9781847945440

Printed and bound in China by
C&C Offset Printing Ltd